Beyond the Mirror:
Volume 5
Dramatic Worlds

Blaze Ward

Knotted Road Press
www.KnottedRoadPress.com

Beyond the Mirror: Volume 5
Dramatic Worlds
Copyright © 2017 Blaze Ward
All rights reserved.
Published 2017 by Knotted Road Press
www.KnottedRoadPress.com

ISBN: 978-1-943663-40-8

Cover art:
© Vantuz | Dreamstime.com - Metal Chrome Retro Microphone On A Stand. Scene With A Red Curta Photo
© Katarzyna Bialasiewicz | Dreamstime.com - Cloudy home - vintage mirror

Cover design and interior design © 2017 Knotted Road Press
www.KnottedRoadPress.com

Never miss a release!
If you'd like to be notified of new releases, sign up for my newsletter. I only send out newsletters once a quarter, will never spam you, or use your email for nefarious purposes. You can also unsubscribe at any time.

http://www.blazeward.com/newsletter/

All rights reserved. No part of this book may be reproduced or transmitted in any form or by any electronic or mechanical means, including information storage and retrieval systems now known or to be invented, without permission in writing from the publisher, except by a reviewer, who may quote brief passages in a review. Scanning, uploading, and electronic distribution of this book or the facilitation of such without the permission of the publisher is prohibited. Please purchase only authorized electronic editions, and do not participate in or encourage electronic piracy of copyrighted materials. Your support of the author's rights is appreciated. Any member of educational institutions wishing to photocopy part or all of the work for classroom use, or anthology, should send inquiries to Knotted Road Press, 27200 272nd Ave SE, Unit #61, Ravensdale, WA 98051 or email: Info@KnottedRoadPress.com.

CAUTION: Professionals and amateurs are hereby warned that these works are subject to payment of a royalty. The play is fully protected under the copyrights laws of the United States, Canada, United Kingdom, and all British Commonwealth countries, and all countries covered by the International Copyright Union, the Pan-American Copyright Convention, the Universal Copyright Convention, the Berne Convention, and all countries with which the United States of America has reciprocal copyright relations. All rights, including without limitation professional, amateur, motion picture, recitation, lecturing, public reading, radio broadcasting, television, video or sound taping, and all other forms of mechanical or electronic reproduction, transmission and distribution, such as CD, DVD, the Internet, private and file-sharing networks, information storage and retrieval systems and photocopying, and rights of translation into foreign languages, are strictly reserved.

First-class professional, stock, and amateur applications for permission to perform it, and those other rights stated above, must be made in advance to Knotted Road Press, 27200 272nd Ave SE, Unit #61, Ravensdale, WA 98051 (or via email: Info@KnottedRoadPress.com) and by paying the requisite fee, whether the play is presented for charity or gain and whether or not admission is charged.

Also by Blaze Ward

The Jessica Keller Chronicles
Auberon
Queen of the Pirates
Last of the Immortals
Goddess of War

Additional Alexandria Station Stories
The Story Road
Siren

Javier Aritza Stories
The Science Officer
The Mind Field
The Gilded Cage

Doyle Iwakuma Stories
The Librarian
Demigod
Greater Than The Gods Intended

Other Science Fiction Stories
Mymirdons
Moonshot

Fairchild

White Crane

The Collective Universe
Imposters
The Shipwrecked Mermaid

Table Of Contents

Homecomings	1
Two Words	57
Chairs	79
Soapbox Prophesies	89
The Winterstone	99

HOMECOMINGS
A PLAY IN ONE ACT

Characters

The Times

The Reporter. Middle-aged cynic. No longer planning to change the world, but the instincts of a bloodhound never go away.

"Brand" (Brandon) Pierce

The Author. Late Thirty-something. Tall, dark, lean, ascetic. Dressed in black. Glasses. Almost suave. Highly educated. Reasonably successful author/playwright.

"Nash" (Natasha) Strickland

The Ex-wife. Late Thirty-something. Tall, busty, natural blond, lots of curls. Gorgeous and curvy. Something of an airhead.

Stanley Fleming

The Producer. Fifty-something. Father figure to both Brand and Nash from when they were young. Wily and cunning, but good-hearted. Wants his brass ring, but not at the cost of everyone else's soul.

"Lissa" (Melissa) Reynolds

The Girl. Mid-twenties. Short, dark haired, petite. "Mousy" growing up, but lately has come into her own as a woman.

Setting

Stanley's apartment. Decorated with memorabilia from the theater. Entryway. Bar. Living Room. Living room located between Entryway and Bar.

Time

A cocktail party after Opening Night. Late Evening.

SCENE 1

AT RISE: The Bar. TIMES and STANLEY enter together, walk to bar. STANLEY sits on barstool. TIMES begin rifling through bottles.

      TIMES
Stanley, where do you keep the good stuff?

      STANLEY
    (STANLEY ignores TIMES, walks around bar, digs around under the bar, pulls out a bottle, pours a drink. Swallows half of it.)
Well, thank God we made it through that mess.

      TIMES
    (Pours, matching STANLEY drink for drink like old drinking buddies.)
You say that every time one of your plays opens.

STANLEY
And it is always appropriate. Doubly so this time. So, what will the Times say about us?

TIMES
I'm still working on the story. This one has so many potential angles to explore. The return of Brandon Pierce to the stage that first launched him.

STANLEY
That should be 'Triumphant Return.' It's my play, I can say these things.

TIMES
Well, pour me some more of your expensive whiskey to help me think.

STANLEY
Should I light you a cigar with a hundred dollar bill while we're at it?

TIMES
Actually, maybe you should hold onto the cash. The house looked a bit thin.

STANLEY
Damn it. You cannot print that. No one will come to the play. Besides, it was a sellout.

TIMES
How many of those tickets were sold to corporate sponsors who gave them away to employees and friends? How many people actually came? It might have been a sellout, but it certainly wasn't standing room only.

STANLEY
It will be. You just have to give it time.

TIMES
And a good byline. All this seems just a little bit too much 'Dog Bites Man.' I just can't go anywhere with that.

STANLEY
So, we need to create a bit of controversy? Spice things up for your readers?

TIMES
Hmm. Just what did you have in mind?

STANLEY
How about the personal element? Brandon and his ex-wife Nash haven't spoken in several years. This is the first time since the divorce that they've even been in the same room.

TIMES
And how did you manage that?

STANLEY
I'm a wily old veteran. Plus I called in some favors.

TIMES
So what do you expect?

STANLEY
I have no idea, but I'm sure we'll be able to find something to titillate your readers. There is no such thing as Bad Publicity. How about the Romantic Angle?

NASH
(ENTERS.)

STANLEY
Ah, Natasha. We were just talking about you. I'm sure you remember our illustrious representative from the Times. He could use some gossip, but if you two will excuse me, I need to attend to some of my guests.

STANLEY
(EXITS.)

TIMES
So, does this mean you are giving up Hollywood and moving home?

NASH
Don't be absurd. This play is a favor for Stanley.

TIMES
A favor?

NASH
Absolutely. My commercials are doing quite well. The only reason Stanley's paying me anything at all is union rules require it. And I'm giving all that money to a local children's charity. Are you coming to the auction next week?

TIMES
I'm not sure. What about your ex-husband Brand?

NASH
We've never stopped being friends.

TIMES
Even after all those nasty things said during the divorce?

NASH
Silly, you should never read gossip columns. Even the ones you write.

TIMES
Because they don't know the true story?

NASH
Because they have papers to sell, readers to thrill, viewers to dazzle.

TIMES
So what is the truth?

NASH
Oh, something far too inane and banal to interest your readers.

TIMES
You might be surprised. So what was it like returning home, especially to star in a play written by your ex-husband?

NASH
I never realized how much I've missed it. It's so different here from Hollywood. It was like being back in school again.

TIMES
Did you and Brand work together much in college?

NASH
It's where we first met. Where we fell in love. He used to write things just for me in those days. In fact, he wrote this play, 'Midnight at the Silversouth Café' just for me.

BRAND
(ENTERS.)
Nash.

NASH
(Air Kiss.)
Darling, so good to see you. I was just telling the Times about our wonderful time together.

BRAND
Really? Which parts?

NASH
Silly, how I've always been your muse, your inspiration. How the happy ending to the play is because you want me back.

BRAND

Nash, while being divorced from you helps, you are about a foot too tall, and far too blond, to be her.

NASH

Her? Wait. Who?

BRAND

The inspiration behind the play. I thought that's what you two were talking about.

TIMES

This sounds interesting. Who is she then?

BRAND

An angel who touched my soul one night.

TIMES

And then what?

BRAND
(Makes to leave.)

She left.

TIMES
(Grabs his arm.)

Hold on. Where did she go?

BRAND
(Makes to leave, again)

The last time I saw her, she was moving to Philadelphia.

TIMES
(Follows)

Philly, huh? When was that?

BRAND
(Laughs.)
About four years ago. If you hurry, you might catch her.

NASH
(Ignored, stands up and stomps off in a huff. EXITS.)

TIMES
You've got to give me more than that.

BRAND
Let it go, will you?

TIMES
Are you kidding me? "MYSTERY MUSE DISCOVERED." I can see it in two inch letters across the front page. Everyone needs a Pulitzer moment. This could be mine.

BRAND
I'm sure that by now you've read the book. You've seen the play. You know who she is. At least as well as I do.

TIMES
But that's just it. The play leaves out as much as it covers. I need more than that to go on.

BRAND
And why should I give you more?

TIMES
You owe me. Hell, I remember interviewing you six years ago when 'The Winterstone Chronicles' opened.

BRAND
Oh. Yeah. That wasn't exactly a fun time for me.

TIMES

Really? I don't think surly quite conveyed your attitude towards the world in general and this reporter in particular. Contempt, perhaps? Now everything is bright and cheery and I'm supposed to let it go, just like that?

BRAND

Yes. It was a long time ago. People change. Sometimes, even for the better.

TIMES

But, what about--?

BRAND

Look. She wanted her privacy, and I'm honoring that. End of story. Go bug Stanley or Nash for a while.

(Exit BOTH.)

BLACKOUT

SCENE 2

AT RISE: The Living Room. BRAND and NASH are seated comfortably on a sofa. Each holds a drink.

NASH
So how come you never told me about her?

BRAND
You, too? Look, we've been divorced for what? Five years now? You've had two other husbands since me.

NASH
That's not fair. You were always my first love.

BRAND
No, the stage was always your first love. I was never more than a distant second on my best day.

NASH
And when did I ever come ahead of your writing?

BRAND

Probably never. We were two stupid kids who were going to change the world, weren't we?

NASH
(Laughs.)

Aren't they all?

BRAND

I suppose so. But I look around and I see how much has changed. Being unhappy made me rich and successful. Being neurotic made you famous.

NASH
(Starts to stand.)

Neurotic? Look, you--

BRAND

Hold on just a minute, Nash. I was married to you for ten years. You were never out of character, even when you were asleep. You're in character right now.

NASH
(Again rises to leave.)

You have no call to--

BRAND

I don't say this to be mean. It's just that I don't think we ever really talked, even when we were married. And we've barely said anything to each other except through your attorneys in more than half a decade.

NASH

You want to relive those days again? Make up for lost time?

BRAND

Oh, Lord, no. That was a very long time ago and a place I don't want to go back to. I found a way to finally be happy, and I am. What about you? Are you happy being you?

NASH
I don't know...

BRAND
That's just another way of saying no.

NASH
But I--... I don't think I know how.

BRAND
Neither did I. But things happen, life happens, and all your assumptions change, and you find a way. I've known you for a very long time, so I hope I can tell you this as a friend. When you are ready for it, happiness will find you.

BRAND
(Stands.)
Your glass is empty. Let me get you another.

NASH
But I--, I--, I--... Yes. Okay. Brand? Thank you.

BRAND
(Exits left.)

LISSA
(Enters right.)

LISSA
(Holds out script and pen.)
Ms. Strickland, can I get your autograph? Are you okay?

NASH
I'm fine. I always have time for my public.

LISSA
If this is a bad time...?

NASH

On the contrary, I think that it's turning out to be a good night, after all. What's your name?

LISSA

This is for my mother. Please make it to Stacy.

NASH

(Hands her signed script.)

Here you go. A big fan of mine, is she?

LISSA

Actually, she's really a big fan of Brandon. She volunteers as an usher at the theater and had to stay late, so she asked me to come.

NASH

Brand, huh? Well you are both in luck tonight.

LISSA

How so?

NASH

He's around here somewhere. You'll be able to get his autograph as well.

LISSA

Really? I mean, he is? Uhm. My-- uh-- mother will really appreciate that. I understand that you were married to Brandon once?

NASH

Some of the happiest times of my life. We both started out right here together. Did you know that I was his muse when we were married?

LISSA

I'd heard that. But I've really only become familiar with his work in the last few years.

NASH
Things are different now that he's moved back to the sticks. We lost touch.

LISSA
Do you miss him?

NASH
Occasionally. But I've been married to two other wonderful men, and my career in LA is poised to take off just as soon as I get home.

LISSA
You're only here for the play?

NASH
Oh, heavens yes. Just a favor for my old friend Stanley. He gave me my first big break, back when I was a wide-eyed innocent, seduced by the bright lights and big stage.

LISSA
No regrets?

NASH
In this business, there's no time for regrets. You just learn what you can from mistakes and move on. If you dwell on the bad things, all you get are wrinkles.

LISSA
I'll keep that in mind. Good luck when you get home.

NASH
Thank you. Don't lose that signature, it's going to be worth a lot of money one of these days.

(Exit both.)

BLACKOUT

SCENE 3

AT RISE: The Bar. LISSA seated at Bar with half-empty glass. TIMES enters, walks up to the bar and rifles through all the bottles at the bar until he finds the expensive stuff hidden in back. Grabs a highball glass, pours several fingers neat.

        TIMES
      (Toasts the room and empties glass.)
To 'Good Mysteries.'

        LISSA
What's that? Good mysteries?

        TIMES
      (TIMES makes to refill her glass, but LISSA stops him. TIMES leans in, conspiratorial.)
Indeed. The mystery tonight, as I've been able to piece it together, is that after he and Nash got divorced, Brand ran off with some other woman, had a whirlwind affair, and she completely turned his life around.

LISSA

A woman did that?

TIMES

Well, sure. This the same guy who wrote 'The Last Train to Dublin' and 'The Winterstone Chronicles.' Very dark and tragic stuff. Mind you, they were incredibly successful novels and even turned out to be pretty good plays. But 'Midnight at the Silversouth Café' is just so completely different that some people have a hard time adjusting.

LISSA

And you think a woman is responsible? Who is she?

TIMES

That's the maddening part. Brand won't tell me. And no one else seems to know she even existed before tonight.

LISSA

He never told anyone?

TIMES

So far, all I know is that she's short, not blond, and lived in Philadelphia four years ago.

LISSA

That's not much to go on.

TIMES

No, but it's a good mystery. And it beats writing another dull story about a half-way interesting play opening in a regional theater.

LISSA

So now you have to pursue this mystery woman and uncover Brand's 'Dark Secret.' Except you have almost nothing to go on and nobody will tell you anything. Have I got it right so far?

TIMES
The night is young.

STANLEY
(Enters off to one side, distracted.)

TIMES
(TOASTS STANLEY.)
And Stanley has good whiskey.

LISSA
(Grabs TIMES arm.)
Did you ever think that maybe it ought to be left alone?

TIMES
Perhaps. But I just can't do that. (Theatrical flourish.) There is a mystery afoot…

LISSA
Ah. Sherlock Holmes, now, are we?

TIMES
Young lady, every reporter is an aspiring crime novelist. Or a failed one.

LISSA
And which are you?

TIMES
The night is young. Here's just the person I need. Stanley, can you explain the importance of 'The Silversouth Café' to this young lady? I have witnesses to interrogate.

TIMES
(Exits.)

STANLEY
What was that lunatic reporter spouting off about?

LISSA
Why is this play such a break from Brand's earlier work?

STANLEY
Ah, yes. Well, it's like this. For the very first time, the hero gets the girl. Revolutionary. At least for Brand.

LISSA
How so?

STANLEY
Take one of his older plays, 'The Last Train to Dublin' for example. That final scene at the train station. The boy's train has already left. She arrives, she's holding his letter, but she's too late. When we produced the adaptation, I wanted to change the ending. Let it go dark with everything just dangling. Her still on the boardwalk, ready to decide. Maybe she goes, maybe she gives up.

LISSA
What happened?

STANLEY
Oh, ho! Brand threw an absolute fit. Threatened to revoke his permission for the work and sue my shorts off.

LISSA
Really? So how did it end?

STANLEY
Just like the book, almost word for word. She stands there, crying, for nearly a minute, and then turns around and slowly walks away as the lights come down. I still think my ending would have worked better. Leave the audience demanding an answer, filling in their own happily-ever-after.

LISSA
But this play has a happy ending. After all the turmoil and accusations, after all the hurt feelings and soul-searching, they leave together.

STANLEY
Yes, I asked him about that. You know, that may have been the first time I ever saw that man smile that didn't involve me writing him a check.

LISSA
Your friend, the reporter, seems to think there was a woman, several years ago, but no one knows who she is.

STANLEY
It confused me as well when I first read 'Midnight at the Silversouth Café.' Tell me, have you even fallen in love at first sight?

LISSA
I came close once, but it didn't work out.

STANLEY
Pity. Well apparently, Brand did. He met her, his new muse, and was swept off his feet. A week later, she was gone, nobody knows where. Nine months later, the 'Silversouth Café' hits the publisher's desk. Six months after that, it hits the Bestseller list. And tonight, the premiere of the play to a sold-out house.

LISSA
But love at first sight?

STANLEY
Apparently, it can even make a cynical curmudgeon like Brand turn over a new leaf. You should try it sometime. Now, if you'll pardon me, I see Brand. Would you care to join me?

LISSA
No, thank you. You go ahead. I think I need another drink first.

STANLEY
(Bows.)

Madame.

                    STANLEY
                    (Exits.)

                    LISSA
                    (Rifles through bottles.)

BLACKOUT

SCENE 4

AT RISE: The Entryway. BRAND pulling on jacket, obviously preparing to leave party. Appears upset. STANLEY enters from apartment-side and moves to intercept him.

STANLEY
Brand, you can't be leaving already.

BRAND
I have had more than enough, thank you.

STANLEY
But the party's just getting started.

BRAND
You haven't had that obnoxious reporter chasing after you all night.

STANLEY
Well, I understand that there's a story to be had.

BRAND
Not you, too. God, I'm sorry that it ever came up.

STANLEY
What do you mean? This is fabulous.

BRAND
I'm not going to get away from your friendly reporter if I stay here. I've seen hungry bulldogs with less focus. Now everywhere I go, people want to talk about the 'Mystery Woman' behind 'Midnight at the Silversouth Café.'

STANLEY
Well, I must admit, it makes an even better story than you and Nash meeting again for the first time in years. We were really expecting more fireworks there. Frankly, that's been a bit of a disappointment.

BRAND
You and the Times are in this together?

STANLEY
Of course we are. Brand, if we play this right tonight, you'll be front page news all week. We'll be playing to a packed house for months.

BRAND
Damn it, Stanley. You have no right to pry into my life like that.

STANLEY
You listen here, young man. I'm doing this because we need the coverage. We need the Times. We need the press stirring things up. We need your fans in an absolute lather over the next revelation. Otherwise, this play is going to flop and cost me a lot of money. Now, you might have all the cash you need tucked away, but if this play doesn't do much better than this, I am going to be ruined.

BRAND
Better? But tonight was a sell-out.

STANLEY
Don't let the press releases fool you. Nearly a quarter of the tickets sold tonight were because I leaned on my sponsors, bothered my friends, and called in every favor anyone owes me. Otherwise, it could have been half empty out there. Now, maybe, people reading the paper will see that it was a sell-out, so, maybe, they'll decide to come see it, and then, maybe, tell their friends. And maybe not. But a really good story gets everyone wound up, excited, ready to pay good money to find out 'The Truth.'

BRAND
It's all a game? Push everyone's buttons, stir up trouble, make a profit?

STANLEY
Who was it who took a chance on a young, unknown playwright fifteen years ago? People weren't ready for the kinds of dark things you wrote. Nobody wanted anything less than a happy ending in those days. You changed that. You got people talking about how a play should end. Why the boy maybe doesn't deserve the girl. You've turned it completely around. People are not expecting the famous Brandon Pierce to write a happy ending. They come expecting the worst. They want to see the failures of love, playing it safe instead of risking it all on the roll of the dice. Now you want a happy ending?

BRAND
This is my life, you manipulating bastard!

STANLEY
Grow up, Brand. That's how it goes in this game. You've been like a son to me and I want to see you succeed. But right now, you need to stand up and take this like a man.

BRAND
(Makes to leave.)
Forget it. I've had enough of the crap around here. I'm going home.

STANLEY
Now look here. If you walk out the door right now, this play won't last a week. It'll close, and take me down with it. And then no one will touch you with a pole. You'll end up writing Mexican soap operas if you aren't careful.

BRAND
That's harsh, even from you.

STANLEY
Please, Brand, I'm asking this as a friend. I need your help.

BRAND
All this because you need my help? Did asking never cross your mind?

STANLEY
I had no idea that the mystery woman story would get that reporter so riled up. I was hoping for a big to-do on whether you and Nash would be getting back together. All the usual crap you read in the Entertainment Section. That would have stirred up enough young romantics around here to keep us in business. Now we've got a love-triangle going. It could be huge. Imagine a house full of potential groupies.

BRAND
Stanley, you are an absolute shit. I don't want groupies. (Smiles in spite of himself.) But remind me never to play poker with you.

STANLEY
(Exits. Dialogue fades.)
Poker? Ha! Did I ever tell you about the time when I...

BRAND
(Exits.)

BLACKOUT

SCENE 5

AT RISE: The Living room. BRAND and NASH seated on sofa with drinks as Scene 2.

NASH
Brand, do you ever wonder?

BRAND
Wonder?

NASH
How it might have turned out?

BRAND
How what might have turned out?

NASH
Us.

BRAND

What us?

NASH

Silly. "Us" us.

BRAND

Nash, there hasn't been an "us" in a long time.

NASH

But we had something. Once. Once upon a time…

BRAND

We're not twenty anymore.

NASH

I know that.

BRAND

So what do you want?

NASH

I don't know.

BRAND

Then what are you smiling about?

NASH

I was thinking about that trip we took in college to the Shakespeare festival in Oregon.

BRAND

What about it?

NASH

The drive across country. I'd never even been out of the state before. It was all this fabulous adventure. Never knowing what we might see, or even where we would sleep. I miss the freedom, the sunrises, those carefree, silly kids. What ever happened to them?

BRAND
They grew up, got married, and ran away to Hollywood.

NASH
That's it?

BRAND
It was enough, until the day when the boy came home and found the girl in bed with someone else.

NASH
That's why you wouldn't talk to me for two years?

BRAND
Things were going well for you out there. Not so for me. A few screenplays, the occasional script, a lot of nothing. My books and plays from the old days were all that kept me going.

NASH
You could have said something.

BRAND
You were never listening. After a while, I gave up talking.

NASH
And left.

BRAND
There was nothing left to say. I was barely working, absolutely miserable, and apparently superfluous.

NASH
You could have tried harder…

BRAND
You aren't listening. God, you weren't listening then either.

NASH
What happened?

BRAND
Why is it so important?

NASH
Because I still care about you. (Pause.) And you never let me say I was sorry.

BRAND
I came home, and started over.

NASH
And wrote this play.

BRAND
Well, the book first.

NASH
But what happened? You never used to believe in happy endings. It was always tragedy and anger with you. Something changed.

BRAND
(Laughs.)
Are you sure you and that reporter aren't working together? I met someone. She showed me that it was okay to believe in happy endings.

NASH
A girl.

BRAND
Are you jealous?

NASH
No! Maybe. Did she make you happy?

                        BRAND

Happy?

NASH
If I couldn't make you happy, what did she do?

                        BRAND

She left.

                        NASH

Left?

                        BRAND

I moved in on a Wednesday. Met her on a Friday. The following Thursday, she moved to Philadelphia.

                        NASH

You let her go?

                        BRAND

She was already leaving when I met her. That Friday was her going-away party.

                        NASH

But just like that, she left?

                        BRAND

Just like that.

                        NASH

And then what?

                        BRAND

Then nothing. End of story.

                        NASH

Didn't you at least try to get her to stay?

BRAND
Sure. But once someone has made up their mind, talking them out of it is rarely anything but a disservice.

NASH
So it was just a quick fling? A three-day affair and then on to your next lover?

BRAND
We never slept together. Well, once, but we were fully clothed the whole time.

NASH
So you never...?

BRAND
We were never lovers. I would have liked that but it never happened. And there was no one after that.

NASH
But-- How? Why?

BRAND
It was her choice and I accepted that. After she left, I was depressed for a while but then I woke up one morning and decided I was ready to move on with my life. I wrote 'Midnight at The Silversouth Café,' turned it into a play, convinced Stanley to make it. He brought you in. And here we are.

NASH
There's been no one else since then?

BRAND
Good lord, you really are jealous, aren't you?

NASH
No. Maybe. Why not?

                    BRAND
Because I could only handle having my heart broken twice.

                    NASH
Twice? Oh. I'm so sorry, Brand. I never meant for things to turn out this way.

                    BRAND
Water under the bridge.

                    LISSA
                    (Enters. Stands in background unseen by principles.)

                    NASH
Do you ever miss me?

                    BRAND
Sometimes. Once upon a time, you were my muse.

                    NASH
But not anymore?

                    BRAND
You were a dark and terrible angel.

                    NASH
That's a horrid thing to say. I thought you loved me.

                    BRAND
I did.

                    NASH
But not anymore?

                    BRAND
Nash, that was a long time ago.

NASH

What about us?

BRAND

Once the play is done, you'll go back to LA. I'll stay here. That is how the story ends.

NASH

Does it have to be that way?

BRAND

I'm not your keeper. I'm just your ex-husband. You're an adult. You can screw up your own life.

NASH

So you're going to shut me out? Again?

BRAND

What is it you want?

NASH

I don't know. (Thoughtful pause.) Can we try again?

BRAND

No. I'm not going through that again.

NASH

That's it?

BRAND

No, that's not "it." I mean, I suppose we could start fresh. After all this time, when you really look at it, we're just two strangers who've met at a party.

NASH

Just like when we were nineteen.

BRAND
Just like that. Hi, I'm Brandon.

NASH
I'm Natasha. (Hugs him.) Oh, Brand, I've missed you.

LISSA
(Exits still unseen.)

BRAND
I need to get something to drink. Don't go anywhere.

BRAND
(Exits.)

STANLEY
(Enters.)

STANLEY
Natasha, you look positively radiant. Is everything alright?

NASH
It's so good, I'm bubbling over.

STANLEY
Well, share your bounty.

NASH
Brand wants me back!

STANLEY
Oh. I see. He said… Really?

NASH
Isn't it wonderful?

STANLEY
It would seem so. I thought you were planning on going home in a month or so.

NASH
I am. Now I've just got to convince him to come with me. It'll be just like before.

STANLEY
I rather suspect it would.

NASH
I'm so happy. You'll talk to Brand, won't you?

STANLEY
I will most certainly discuss this with him, my dear. We were just talking about poker a few minutes ago.

NASH
What's that?

STANLEY
Nothing. Consider it done, my dear.

NASH
Oh, Stanley. I knew I could count on you.

STANLEY
Anything for you. But Natasha, what if he wants to stay here?

NASH
Why would he want to do that? We'll be together. He said so.

STANLEY
Together. He said that?

NASH
Well, he's willing to start fresh. It's easy from there. (Cleavage shimmy.) No man can resist my charms.

STANLEY
Oh, I have no doubt. It's just...

NASH
What?

STANLEY
Do you really love him?

NASH
What do you mean?

STANLEY
It's been four years, Natasha.

NASH
So?

STANLEY
You've had two other husbands.

NASH
Neither of them could measure up to Brand.

STANLEY
Then why on earth did you marry them?

NASH
Jerry reminded me so much of Brand when we met. It was such as shame that it didn't work out. And Eric actually wrote a part for me in his show. That was so sweet.

STANLEY
So now you want Brand.

NASH
It will be just like college again.

STANLEY
Ah. The dreams of youth die the hardest.

NASH
What do you mean?

STANLEY
You've both changed so much since I first met you. Are you sure you want to try to be twenty again?

NASH
Stanley, every girl wants to be twenty forever.

STANLEY
Are you really sure what you want?

NASH
We'll be the toast of the town, all the best parties.

STANLEY
Brand seems happy here.

NASH
He'll be happier there.

STANLEY
What if there is someone else?

NASH
He told me there has been no one since me. Don't you see? That means he's still waiting for me, pining for me.

STANLEY
What about the rumor floating around about...

NASH
Her? Nothing. A cheap fling. No woman can compete with this.

STANLEY
Natasha, there is more to life than tits and ass.

NASH
That just goes to show how little you really know about this business.

STANLEY
So you'll just swoop into his life and stake a claim?

NASH
He's obviously confused, hiding out here in the sticks.

STANLEY
I see. Maybe you should go slow.

NASH
This is no time to go slow. I need to get him hooked quickly.

STANLEY
I'll talk to him.

NASH
I knew I could count on you, Stanley.

STANLEY
(Exits.)

NASH
(Exits.)

BLACKOUT

SCENE 6

AT RISE: The Bar. BRAND seated at bar, enjoying a cocktail. LISSA enters.

BRAND

Lissa?

LISSA

Hello, Brand.

BRAND

I'm not dreaming?

LISSA

No, I'm real.

BRAND

I was afraid that I'd never--

LISSA
For the longest time, you weren't meant to.

BRAND
You never said forever.

LISSA
I hadn't planned it that way. When I got settled, I found one of your books. It was dark and depressing. I couldn't handle it. I didn't want to be around someone that bleak and angry.

BRAND
So what changed?

LISSA
I made the mistake of telling my mother about you. Now she has all your books. She tells me constantly that I should get back in touch with you.

BRAND
You know, I've dreamed this scene hundreds of times.

LISSA
How did it turn out?

BRAND
I never really believed that you'd come back. You never answered my letters. Either you wanted to see me again, or you didn't.

LISSA
Stanley and I talked about love at first sight.

BRAND
What about it?

LISSA
I nearly let it happen that night.

BRAND
Nearly?

LISSA
Most of me was already gone.

BRAND
So it meant nothing?

LISSA
Oh, God, no. There were so many times I wanted to chuck it all and call you.

BRAND
But you never did.

LISSA
Brand, I'd spent my whole life trying to escape this town, this life, these people. I was afraid you'd drag me back. You were the perfect gentleman, telling me about places you'd been, things you'd seen, people you'd known. I wanted a chance to make my own stories.

BRAND
Did you?

LISSA
I was starting to when I read 'The Winterstone Chronicles.'

BRAND
Ouch. Bad choice. I was not in a happy place when I wrote that one.

LISSA
I know that. Now. But I could only see the hurt, the need. I was afraid of becoming a moth to a flame. I needed to find myself, to discover my own strength. I didn't want to turn back into another follower.

BRAND

Lissa, I--

LISSA

So there I was. New town, new life. Good job, a nice apartment, the occasional date. But I couldn't stop thinking about you.

BRAND

You could have called, written, anything.

LISSA

It was one night. One utterly perfect, completely strange night, listening to the rain, cuddling in front of the fireplace. We kissed once. How big of an impression could I have made?

BRAND

Big enough.

LISSA

But how? I've read 'Midnight at the Silversouth Café,' but I still don't understand.

BRAND

Maybe it's because you left.

LISSA

What?

BRAND

For one night, I got to hold someone who had no axe to grind, no demons to battle, no angle to exploit. When the bar closed that night, we went our separate ways. I thought that was the end of the story.

LISSA

But it wasn't.

BRAND
I had gotten home just barely long enough to take off my shoes when the doorbell rings.

LISSA
It could have been a stalker.

BRAND
She didn't know where to find me then.

LISSA
She?

BRAND
Another time, maybe. So there you were, soaking wet. It was my duty, my pleasure to keep you warm and safe.

LISSA
But I wanted more, I think.

BRAND
Probably, but I would have scared you off if anything had happened.

LISSA
Oh. Maybe. But still--

BRAND
And then you left. No fights, no tears. Just one kiss.

LISSA
All this from that kiss?

BRAND
No. There was hope, depression, the whole Kubler-Ross thing.

LISSA
You went through the stages of death?

BRAND

Something like that. Then something strange happened. Nothing. I was left with only happy memories of you. Nothing harsh or angry. No bitter words, no betrayals. So I started writing again.

LISSA

"Midnight at the Silversouth Café."

BRAND

No, that came later. This was after I had decided that you were gone for good.

LISSA

So what was it?

BRAND

I started writing a modern Iliad. You were Helen, but I couldn't be Paris or Agamemnon.

LISSA

So who were you?

BRAND

I'm not sure. Paris would never go to the ends of the earth for Helen, while Agamemnon was perfectly willing to destroy everything that got in his way. Perhaps Odysseus.

LISSA

So that would make me Penelope?

BRAND

Well, there was always the hope that you were pining away.

LISSA

But I left you behind.

BRAND

OK, bad metaphor. You can be Odysseus and I'll be Penelope. The point is, all the anger was gone. It was like night had set and left me the cool light of morning. That's when I wrote the Silversouth Café. I couldn't think of any other way to send you a message in a bottle.

LISSA

Did you really have to use my name for the main character?

BRAND

If I'd named her anything else, you might not have listened. It's not like it mattered to more than two people in the whole world. Excuse me, three, counting your mother.

LISSA

You knew I'd see it and contact you?

BRAND

Knew? No. Hoped? Absolutely.

(EVERYONE else enters from different directions. Stand silently watching.)

LISSA

So if I'm Odysseus returning home to find my beloved, are there any suitors in your hall that I must slay to win your affections back?

NASH
(Steps up.)

Only one.

STANLEY
(To TIMES.)

Tell me you're getting all of this.

TIMES
(To STANLEY.)

Recorder's been running most of the night.

STANLEY
Good. No more complaints about being bored.

TIMES
Wouldn't think of it. Wait a minute. She's "Her"?

STANLEY
For a reporter, you can be amazingly dense at times.

TIMES
(Grunts and starts writing notes.)

LISSA
(Turns to NASH.)
Don't you think it's about time you came clean? I heard you talking to Stanley. Going to swoop in and "rescue" poor Brand from a life of obscurity in the middle of nowhere? Take him back to the West Coast? Dazzle him with the bright lights and empty promises?

NASH
That's certainly more that you've got to offer, Twiggy. This time I'll make it work. You watch. We'll be the toast of the town.

LISSA
What if he wants to stay here? Maybe even be happy?

NASH
What would you know about making him happy? Or any man, for that matter?

LISSA
Based on what I've heard here tonight, a lot more than you.

NASH
You can't have him.

LISSA
You make him sound like a prize.

NASH
Well, he's my prize. Besides, you left.

LISSA
Yes, I did. And you should have. Don't you ever think of anyone besides yourself?

NASH
I want what's best for Brand.

LISSA
Really?

BRAND
(Steps into conversation.)

STANLEY
(Moves to intervene.)
Brand--

BRAND
Shut up, Stanley.

STANLEY
No. And stop glaring at me like that. I can tell by the look on your face that you're about to say something you'll probably regret. Or worse, maybe you won't.

BRAND
Don't you think you've done enough damage for one night?

STANLEY
Probably. That's why I'm trying to stop this from spiraling entirely out of control.

BRAND
It's far too late for that at this point.

> BRAND
> (Turns to LISSA.)

I can promise you that this didn't go remotely how I hoped. There should have been music and candles. Dancing. Fireworks.

> LISSA

I'm sorry, too.

> BRAND

We'll get through it.

> BRAND
> (Turns to NASH.)

You, on the other hand…

> NASH

Brand, honey, I just want it to be like it was.

> BRAND

That's the problem. It would be. You haven't changed one bit.

> NASH

Of course not. I want it be like it was, forever.

> BRAND

Well, you don't always get what you want.

> NASH

But I'm willing to take you back.

> BRAND

Silly of me to think you'd change. You won't. You can't. But I can't go back there.

> NASH

You mean won't.

BRAND

Same thing. I like being happy.

NASH

But we would be. Don't you see? Haven't you missed all the excitement and glory?

BRAND

No. And if you can't figure that out, then there's nothing left to say.

NASH

What about your promise?

BRAND

I promised to give you a chance. To start over. That means a clean slate. It also means that you have to meet me somewhere in the middle.

NASH

And live here again? Please. Have you any idea what that would do to my career?

BRAND

I can guess. Those are the only terms I'm willing to offer. Take them or leave them.

NASH

We'll just see about that.

NASH
(Exits.)

LISSA

What about us?

BRAND

Any other night, I would have said "Welcome home" and probably offered you my soul. Tonight's different.

LISSA
So, nothing?

BRAND
Princess, I'm all out of glass slippers.

LISSA
I don't need Prince Charming.

BRAND
Are you back? For good?

LISSA
Not yet.

BRAND
When you are, you know how to find me.

BRAND
(To STANLEY.)
How about we just call it even?

BRAND
(Exits.)

STANLEY
(Nods agreement and follows BRAND out.)

LISSA
(Hangs head and follows BRAND and STANLEY out.)

TIMES
(DIALS PHONE.)
Tom? It's me. Yeah. No, good. Look, can we still make the morning edition? Yes? OK, write this down…

DARKNESS

CURTAIN

TWO WORDS
A MONOLOGUE IN ONE ACT

Characters

Max

Male. Mid-30's. American.

Setting

Prologue: The Darkness
Scene 1: The Diner
Scene 2: The Bar
Scene 3: The Highway
Epilogue: The Darkness

Time

Late night.

PROLOGUE

AT RISE: Empty space.

MAX

No, this is the time for you to listen, while I talk. A lot of things have been said tonight. Some of them we even meant, and some we didn't. At this point, I can't tell which ones are which, but that doesn't really matter. When I'm done, you just have to say two words. Nothing more. Nothing less.

First, you can say "Stay tonight." We'll forget all of this nonsense and pretend like it never happened. Tomorrow we'll start off as if none of these words were said, and we'll be back to where we were yesterday. I'll still love you. You'll still love me. We'll look back on tonight as some god-awful nightmare, but we won't dwell on it, except to maybe laugh at what terrible fools we were and how close we came to busting up a good thing.

Second, you can say "Maybe later." I'll grab my things and go away, while you figure out what it is you want. And I'll give you space to sort it out in your own head while I go sort it out in mine. The things that have been said will stay said, and we'll mean them. But maybe we won't be limited by them. Maybe tomorrow, maybe next week, you'll call me and we'll talk. Maybe we'll start over. Maybe we'll just walk away. Maybe we'll keep going and figure it out as we go. I can't predict the future or I'd be wearing better suits. But it won't matter. We're adults. We'll handle this like grownups. Not like two love-struck kids going down in a blaze of terrible glory.

Finally, you can say "Godspeed, Roland." I'll grab my things and go, but this will be different. When I walk out that door, I'll be gone. I won't ever look back, except to shake my head. If you say those terrible words, that will be the end. It's like cutting a rope. You can try to splice it together later if you change your mind and have the patience. You can tie a knot in the two frayed ends and call it good enough, but you've still cut the rope. There are two separate pieces of what used to be a single whole. We'll no longer be an "us," just a "you" here, and a "me" somewhere else. You might even look, but you'll never find me. Because I'll be done. I'll be seeking the Black Tower and a destiny that doesn't include you and has no space in it for us. Even if you do find me, it won't work. We'll just be two strangers meeting on the street. You'll wave. I'll nod. We'll go on our way like friendly strangers do.

There it is. I don't like it, but everything about us can be summed up thus. Three choices. Two words. One decision. My fate is in your hands, because I don't want you to come back later and think that I've made you do something against your will. That will never work. It'll just hang over us and poison things like a bad smell. It's up to you at this point. You say two words, and I'll handle the rest.

(Transition to Diner.)

SCENE 1

AT RISE: The Diner.

MAX

You know, she never said anything. Just kind of stood there and goggled at me. It reminded me of a goldfish I had when I was a kid. Those same mournful, unblinking eyes staring back at me. Her mouth opened and closed, opened and closed, but no sound came out. I thought of cheeks pushing water past gills: a big, round, crystal fishbowl sitting on my father's sideboard, next to his old pipe and a fresh bag of tobacco, today's mail, and yesterday's knick-knacks. Kind of an impromptu inventory of our lives, written in cheap plastic kitsch.

I suppose that, in the end, we're all victims of the accumulation of our yesterdays. She certainly was. It can be raw, I know, when someone you think likes you suddenly reaches up and rips the veil from your face. Everything you thought you knew turns out to be a fat, old man behind a curtain.

But she never said anything. And there is only so long you can stand there not saying anything before it becomes obvious that you haven't got anything to say. Especially when it's all been sorted out for you, like freshly laundered socks, and all you have to do is pick. It's not like a game of three-card monty here. You know what the cards are. And which one you need to pick to win. Assuming you want to win. Or at least know what losing looks like.

So I stood there for a while, wondering if she had been turned into alabaster, or maybe salt. But you can only handle so many ticks of that old grandfather clock before that blind, goldfish stare gets to you. And it got to me. At that point, I had my own choices to make. Lucky for me, she left me in silence to contemplate them. Much faster than contemplating my sins, or I'd still be there counting rosary beads.

I had it easy. If she was going to tell me to stay, it would have come out of her mouth quickly. She'd have kissed my forehead and told me to forget all this foolishness. We might have even managed a few happily-ever-afters before morning.

And if it was going to be the Black Tower for me, I'd have liked to think that she would have already been there too, at least in her own mind. Lord knows she's pretty enough to be Helen. And probably mean enough. Certainly she could have sent me off to sack Troy. And let's face it, not even Achilles was bullet-proof, when you get down to brass tacks.

So that doesn't leave me with a whole lot of other choices to pick from. My momma didn't raise any stupid boys. A couple of dull ones, but none that are positively dumb. All I had left at that point was to depart with at least a modicum of dignity. So I grabbed my hat, tipped it to her, and made it out the door before she could say anything I'd live to regret. Hell, for all I know, she's still standing there, staring at a closed door, waiting for me to rush back through it, grab her, and smother her with kisses. One big happy world. I should have you go check on her; see if she's okay and give her the benefits of your worldly wisdom and woman's intuition.

Except I'm not sure what I want her to do at this point. If you'd have asked me an hour ago, I'd have gone all in on the happily-ever-after part, especially the naughty bits. I'd like to think that all the things that led up to this moment would have meant something. But I piled them up on one side of the scale and watched them turn to pixie dust. Don't get me wrong. That happens to all of us eventually. But I just wasn't prepared to come face to face with that ghost tonight. Maybe Ebenezer can handle it but he had the writers on his side. I'm not so lucky.

If all that means nothing, then cut me loose. Sometimes I feel like bait here. Wriggling on the hook to see if something more enticing happens along to make a snack out of me and a meal for her. But nobody ever asks the worm what he wants from life; it's just cold water, darkness, and sharp hooks.

I might not ever find the Black Tower, but damn it, it's not fair to never even let me try. And right now, I can't love her or hate her. All I've got is a lonesome, flashing yellow street light, an all-night diner, and half a slice of coffee to keep me going.

Religion won't do me any good at this point, either. God himself would be hard pressed to hang me on the horns of a greater dilemma. And Job's got nothing on me after this. But I have to warn you right now lady, that if any of your flora ignites, I'm throwing my coffee on it and running like hell for the highway. All I've got to look forward to now is Revelations and none of them excite me.

Bless me, Father, for my sins are so great that the table of contents alone would keep you here most of the night. I might love a woman, if I can get past the hating her bit, or at least balance the scales with some fresh pixie dust. She might be the Eve to my Adam, although I'm not sure I haven't gotten them backwards to the point where I'm the one talking to snakes. Or at least listening to them. It might be the same thing, because nobody really, honestly, wants to hear the truth, the whole truth, and all the rest of that noise. The parts that aren't dreary and boring turn puerile pretty quick and the rest are still prosecutable, at least until the statute of limitations runs out on some of my more interesting ideas.

But what's your story? Anybody ever boil it down for you that starkly? Trust me, it's a nasty mirror. Looking into it just reminds you that ennui and entropy are kissing cousins, and the whiskey only makes them pretty while it lasts.

(Transition to BAR.)

SCENE 2

AT RISE: The Bar.

MAX

Speaking of which, barkeep, can you set me up with a whiskey? Make it a double. Oh, hell, set up three shots and we'll celebrate Freud's trinity tonight. Because, let's face it, the old boy did get that part right. For what is a man but the sum of his wants and needs? No man is going to be happy unless he has someone to help him with the emotional as well as the physical and the intellectual. Lucky indeed the man who can find all that in one place. And rare as well but we all have our crosses to bear.

Really like that girl, but I'm getting tired of always being kept at fingertip-length. It's not even arm's length any more, although you'd think that by now I'd have gotten used to it. When a woman keeps you at arm's length at first, there's a built-in expectation that eventually she will either warm up to you and bring you closer, or tell you to hit the road. We've all been there. I've got the ex-wives to prove it. But instead of letting me in or throwing me out, she's pushed me back just exactly as far as she can without growing longer finger-nails. And the porch is a cold, lonely place on a night like this.

I may not be a rocket scientist, but I played one once in a commercial, so I understand unstable orbits. And hey, I even passed a few math classes, once upon a time, so I can talk about eccentricity without sounding like a total fool, even if nobody around here would ever mistake me for an egghead. I suppose that as long as no one thinks I'm a nerd, I should count that as a victory. But I'm still trapped in a wobbly place, wandering in the darkness like a lost comet, bullied by big, mean planets I can't even see from here. Moses would feel at home.

So buddy, I'm fresh out of ideas. My father always told me that if you aren't part of the solution, then most likely you'll end up being part of the problem. I'm afraid that that just might be the case here. She sure hasn't been treating me like the cure for what ails her. Where does that leave me? Just another victim of circumstance, standing idly by the side of the road, watching that parade go by.

You know, someone might at the least throw some beads or candy at me, to let me pretend that I'm at Mardi Gras. We could all be in costumes. Or, anyway, better costumes. Certainly more interesting ones. We could take all this commotion and turn it into a proper masquerade. That way, we could be honest about the disguises we're wearing and the roles we're impersonating. And if things don't work out, nobody's really surprised when you swap masks and try something else. And when the fairy godmother taps you on the shoulder and says, "It's midnight, Cinderella," you know what to expect. Everyone will play their part in a predictable fashion and, if you're really lucky, the whole Prince Charming thing doesn't turn out to be a fable after all. And if it does, well at least you've got the shoe to back up one hell of a story. It also makes a pretty good shot glass on those nights when you know that you really shouldn't be drinking the whiskey straight from the bottle but your legs are too rubbery to carry you to the kitchen.

Truth be told, I'm not even sure where all this vitriol came from tonight. It's not like me to think or talk with such ruckus. I'm normally much more of a thinker. Even my wild gambles are carefully considered long before ever hammer strikes iron. But something got into me tonight that I can't rightly explain. It just erupted out of the depths and splattered collateral damage all over the room. I suppose that my only saving grace now is that it came out like Mauna Loa and not Krakatau. It's a lot more controllable that way, when you can mostly get out of the way of things and let them ooze down to the sea, rather than some sudden detonation that turns skies dark and summers cold.

I thought I had put those days long behind me. Hell, even the survivors have mostly forgotten the details now, it's been so long. They just have stories to frighten children. I won't apologize for what I did in those days, but we've all grown a lot older and with any luck a mite wiser. The past is generally dead and mostly buried these days. If you take the right turns and the moon's just right, you can even drive by some of the more interesting spots. Kind of like 'Homes of the Hollywood Stars,' without any famous people.

Not that you'd want to be out on a night like this. The winds are really getting a good run out there, turning that eerie quiet into a thwarted ban sidhe. Not a pleasant woman to come chasing you in the dark. She's pursued me many times, but usually from the warm confines of a screaming nightmare. Tonight, she's almost close enough to feel her clutching your hair as you flee. Don't look around. Just run and hope you don't trip.

Back home, my pop used to call those days "flat rocks." He said you really had two choices when it comes to living. Round rocks make one hell of a big splash, rile things up, and get everything in motion. But then they sink clean out of sight, never to be heard from again. He always said you should try to be a flat rock instead. Them's the ones that can skip clear across the creek on a quiet day, and if you get really lucky, make it to the far shore where you can get them for the next try. And even if they don't quite make it, they'll be close enough that you can wade in and salvage them. I got a few friends like that, willing to wade out to save me, but ain't none of them can swim.

So the lesson I learned from him was to keep your head down, follow through smoothly, and keep the ripples to a minimum. Works as well in stickball as it does in life. The first few skips are always big, but then they flatten out after a while. If we're lucky, they call that growing up, or at least growing old. Don't see that I want to grow up, because grown-ups never seem to have any fun. Well, not much, anyways. Happily-ever-afters are still pretty good, when you can get them. Of course, if that was going to be an option tonight, I wouldn't be here, sipping your whiskey and bending your ear. And I probably shouldn't be. I ought to be out there with a map, trying to find the right road. I don't mean to invoke Robert Browning tonight, but Ol' Frank Baum just doesn't seem to be working for me. And I'd look plumb silly in a pair of shiny red pumps, especially where I'm going. So with that, I'll bid you adieu and hope to make it back through this way again. Then I can tell you a whole new raft of lies and you can laugh at me some more.

(Transition to Highway.)

SCENE 3

AT RISE: The Highway.

MAX

This is a good night to pile into the car and head it into the darkness. We can explore Rune's Rule, and maybe find Shangri-La. Or, if all else fails, we can always fall back on the old standbys. When I was younger, when it got to be too much, I could always rely on the radio gods to get me through. Just find a comfortable spot on the stoop, turn the radio up and watch the world saunter by. Somewhere along the way, all the anger and madness would boil away, lost in the sunset. We'd be left with whatever muses we encountered as we flipped across stations.

Looking back, if you squint your eyes and tilt your head just right, it all makes a kind of sense. Just trust your fate and your sanity to the whims of the radio. It's like a religious experience, with all the sin and very little of the guilt. You seek a sign, and somewhere between Delphi and Nostradamus you have your message. And if it makes no sense, that's OK. Nothing does when you're a teenager, but it's not supposed to. Being a grownup is when it starts to make sense but by then it's not any fun anymore. But tonight takes me back.

A friend once helped me catalyze this truth, when we were young and stupid. Or at least younger and stupider. He called it Rune's Rule. What he told me was that "if you don't care where you're going, you ain't lost." That's a wonderfully liberating thought, because most of us don't really care. We just want to be someplace that's warm and safe. The home we had when we were kids. The kind of place I can't go to tonight, lest I drag all this baggage in with me, like a happy cat bringing you a prize in the morning. You remember the place: Mom's cookies, blanket forts, the first puppy. All the accoutrements of youth. Innocence lost. I didn't care where I was going in those days, as long as it was away. Children turn into teenage monsters, I was no different. But I had the radio to keep me going, when there was no one else I could trust.

Funny how you can never seem to get there from here. You spend all that time trying to get as far away as you can, and when you finally do, you spend the rest of your life trying to get back. And you never can. Hometowns exist only in the dust you shake from your coat and the memories you carry with you forever. But nights like this thin the boundary. All the fire and madness from those days boils up and it starts to feel familiar. You can't sit still. The diner can't contain it, nor can the bar, so you have to hit the highway and look for tomorrow.

And then, just maybe, the radio gods take pity on you and play that song that takes you to yesterday instead. They are usually an impenetrable distance away. Lost forever, but immortal. All the years melt off, at least for a few chords. And it's a different kind of pain, because it's so far away that you can barely see it. But the song remembers every little bit, especially the parts that hurt the most, and feeds it to you one painful note at a time.

Usually, it brings a smile to your face. Maybe because it's a woman's face and fond recollections. And sometimes because you still can't believe that you actually survived some of the crazy things you did. I should not be sitting here. That I am is a testament to luck and timing, both mostly good. And quite possibly just a touch of karma.

Some of those songs can still bring me to tears, decades after the fact. I still wonder where I might have ended up, but for the Grace of God. Let's face it, my entire life is a story of taking the road less traveled. I'm on one of those roads tonight, wandering in the darkness, and I don't need any more sad songs playing. I think at this point subsisting on silence is a good idea, and the hum of the tires can hypnotize me.

It's been an evening where silences might have better served everyone involved, instead of this gumbo that we've cooked up. Usually, the death of talking is a bad thing, leading to awkward silences and strained looks. People stop talking, and people go astray. There's even an old Scottish word for it that's appropriate. It will even fit on a license plate, so maybe I should get the word 'traik' for myself. I seem to have gotten lost.

This certainly wasn't what I had planned when the sun went down tonight. I had anticipated a lovely evening. A little grub, a beer or three, music, dancing, romance, perhaps even some happily-ever-afters. Instead, we wandered down the wrong path. Light conversation and fencing suddenly morphed into some alien monstrosity I never envisioned. But one word led to another, and before you realize, the conversation has turned into a 47-car pileup splashed across a mile of Jersey Turnpike. At least there were no casualties, other than my dignity and peace of mind. Just a dark night, and the death of talking.

And that's where we leave it off. What should have probably been silence to start could have been solved by the insertion of two words. Instead, we've got a whole lot of empty words cast at a wall, kind of like a verbal Jackson Pollack. And like raw spaghetti, nothing seems to be sticking. More words won't help, because the death of talking leaves us with an exercise in hollow monologues.

So much said, and yet so little.

(Transition to EPILOGUE.)

EPILOGUE

AT RISE: Empty space.

MAX

I don't know what you want me to do. I think I've said it all by now, somewhere far beyond the two words that would have summed it all up. I gave it all into your hands, but you've met me with only silence. I've gone as far as I can take myself. You have to give me something.

Take me and put me. Give me your heart, or at least tell me what I need to do to win it. Lay out for me why it is that I'll never touch your soul, so I can plot a course to the middle ground. I can do that, if I must. Or it will be the horn for me.

Can you hear the flourish? That's the Black Tower calling me. As much as I want to love you, the siren is telling me I should forsake you instead. There are monsters out there. Evil stalks the night, sowing seeds of chaos and madness. Only fire and steel can harvest them. If we are to be, it must be now.

You must learn a new song, one I think you have never known. You must stop being afraid of me. We both know I can hurt you. But I will never do so, save in ignorance. So you must teach me. Learn to share something of yourself. The walls will continue to stand, even if you hang a banner from the highest tower.

Alternatively, it will be the OuterDark, where even the stars have fallen. I will leave my sign, a single handprint burned into the stone beside the gate. You've never seen my standard, so it would mean nothing to you to see it now. The hand will be enough, because you will eventually forget what I look like. The stone will remember my touch long after you have forgotten.

There will not come a morning when you waken to my kiss. That is not a future I would choose, but it is not mine at this point. I cannot make the case. I can only ask for your touch. After tonight, I suppose I should also ask for your forgiveness, for having dropped such a tremendous weight on your shoulders when you never asked for it. I have simply reached the point where I'm afraid you will throw everything away. I could live with that, if I knew it was for the right reasons. But I don't know any more what they are. Nor do you. I have only questions. And you have the answers.

When it started, there were three choices for you to make. Stay tonight. Maybe later. Godspeed, Roland. I need you to say two words. We have reached the point where there is nothing else. Otherwise, it will end, but not with a bang.

(DARKNESS.)

END OF PLAY

CHAIRS
A DIALOGUE IN ONE ACT

SCENE 1

AT RISE: BOY seated in one of two chairs. GIRL walks up.

GIRL
(Points to chair.)
May I?

BOY
Only if you plan on flirting with me in a distracting manner while we wait.

GIRL
Why would I do that?

BOY
Uhm. Cost of doing business?

GIRL
(Interested.)
What kind of business?

BOY
It follows a well-defined capitalist model. You have certain needs. I have an excess of chairs.

GIRL
Didn't your mother ever teach you to be a gentleman?

BOY
Oh, sure. But I never met any interesting women that way. We'd both smile awkwardly, shift uncomfortably, mumble politely, and part anonymously. Much more fun this way.

GIRL
What if I'm not that kind of girl?

BOY
Then you'd have already walked away.

GIRL
So by staying...?

BOY
We're already well into a fun and potentially meaningful relationship.

GIRL
All of this over a chair?

BOY
It's a very nice chair.

GIRL
True, but I'm not sure about the neighbors.

BOY
It's safe. I've been here at least ten minutes and not one of them has tried to bite me yet.

GIRL
That's good. I'm not sure I could maintain witty banter if I had to worry about adventurous furniture.

BOY
It's been my experience that timing is everything in these matters.

GIRL
Ah, so you're something of an expert on picking up strange women in crowded places?

BOY
Oh, no. Rankest amateur. I was referring to the chairs.

GIRL
(Skeptical.)
Really?

BOY
Absolutely. You'd be amazed how important furniture wrangling can be these days. Usually the herd is calm and well-behaved, but any wrong thing can spook 'em. Then you've got a stampede on your hands.

GIRL
Good thing I've got you around to protect me.

BOY
And to think, you could have just kept walking and sat someplace else, completely ignorant of these things.

GIRL
I don't know, Starbucks has chairs that look awfully comfortable.

BOY
Well sure, if you prefer caffeination over conversation.

GIRL
Oh, so you prefer your thrills cerebral rather than physical?

BOY
At least initially. My father always told me "No matter how good it goes, eventually you have to roll over and talk to her."

GIRL
So she also has to give good conversation first thing in the morning? Even before makeup?

BOY
Well, cooking skills are good too, unless you like runny scrambled eggs and burnt toast.

GIRL
All that, and I should make you breakfast, too?

BOY
No, no, no. That's where Starbucks comes in.

GIRL
What about the evils of globalization?

BOY
If you know a local place for that for that first hit, I can be adventurous.

GIRL
Who knew seating could be so important?

BOY
The Chinese. It's all about good *feng shui*.

GIRL
So you're saying that if I want to sit here, I have to be willing to go through all the effort of flirting with you just for the good karma?

BOY
Well, it starts there, but I'm not sure that I'm ready for anything beyond that.

GIRL
Commitment issues?

BOY
My mother warned me about strange women.

GIRL
Dangerous?

BOY
Wicked. Who knows how you might lead me astray.

GIRL
I could always sit way over there and mind my own business.

BOY
It's too late for that. The dialectic has already taken hold. All we can do now is ride it to the bitter end.

GIRL
In the rodeo, that's only eight seconds.

BOY
But then you have a ton of mad cow with separation issues. Do you have any clowns handy?

GIRL
Not a one. Didn't even bring a girlfriend along as a wingman.

BOY
That's probably good. Could have been awkward, me flying solo here.

GIRL

Not feeling that ambitious?

BOY

I only have the one chair. Besides, some guy might have walked by and been jealous that I had two hot chicks and he didn't have any. Marxism's really only good in theory.

GIRL

Oh, so you're the greedy type?

BOY

It's my chair. I should get something for my trouble.

GIRL

What about my needs?

BOY

I'm kind of shy and awkward in social settings. You'd probably have to spell it out for me.

GIRL

Should I hold your hand too?

BOY

Don't you think that's a bit forward?

GIRL

Not for a modern woman. Kissing you, in front of all these strangers, on the other hand, that might be a bit much. Might.

BOY

If I'd have known that was on the menu, I'd have upped the ante.

GIRL

Baby-steps there, cowboy. Don't want to get in too deep too quick.

BOY
Hmm. Well, if bull-riding's out, what about calf-roping?

GIRL
(Bends over, flashes him lots of cleavage.)
Only if you brought the whole Bolivian army, Sundance.

BOY
Probably just as well. I can't swim.

GIRL
Shame. Girl's got to have her standards.

BOY
You know, it's a good thing we're only talking about a chair. Otherwise, I get the feeling I could be in real trouble.

GIRL
(Finally sits in chair.)
John, you are incorrigible.

BOY
Hey, you knew that when you married me.

END OF PLAY

SOAPBOX PROPHESIES
A MONOLOGUE IN ONE ACT

Characters

Max

Male. Mid-30's. American.

SCENE 1

AT RISE: Empty space.

MAX

"Why are you like this?" she asked me. As if I could boil it all down to a quick video demonstration with snappy graphics and cool colours. I'm sure that's just what this bar needs tonight. "Why I Am Like This: The Truth In Ten Quick Minutes." With an intermission followed by "All The Stupid Things I Did To Get Here." That sound you hear is Ebenezer giggling. He has it easy. Three quick visitations and a chance to make it all right. That's the problem with Christmas stories. They can make it all turn out fine in the end.

A wise man once laughed in my face and said, "Son, it never ends. Least not 'til yer dead. And maybe not even then." Which pretty much tells me that we are all going to hell. The only real question is in what order. I'll take my time. But that's not the sort of answer she was looking for to her question. "Why are you like this?" What she wanted to know was what made her so special, that I'd go out of my way to not trust her, when she'd never done anything to me. The correct answer is nothing. But that's the wrong question.

The really important question here is why I should turn things on their head and trust her in the first place. You see, it's the cynic in me. If you approach everything with low expectations, then the only real surprises will be the good kind. I've known too many of those dark, nasty, dead-cold, four-in-the-morning ones. You know the kind. Wake up from a dead sleep with a sudden "What the hell am I doing here?" bursting from your lips. It's far less embarrassing when you're sleeping alone, but that's not usually when it happens now, is it?

No, you're far more likely to be waking someone else up when you have one of those dreams that sets your heart to pounding and the cold sweat to running, while the moon is high and the sun is just starting to think about maybe rattling itself out of bed. It's cold, and dark, and only one lonely streetlight in the distance breaks it up. And you have to try to explain it to someone. Times like these, I'm not sure Crime Alley wouldn't be preferable, considering.

But we're not here to analyze my dreams, thank God. The inkblots can keep my secrets a bit longer, while we wander the intrepid darkness asking about Trust™. I suppose that it comes down to the fundamental differences between woman and man. Or at least what bits I've been able to scrape together and call wisdom. For verisimilitude's sake, we'll leave it at that tonight and be happy.

At the end of the day, all too often, a man sees his glass as half full, while a woman looks at him and see's that it's really half empty. Ladies, we're generally simple creatures, driven by primitive wants and needs; lusts and fears. Fragile most times. Egomaniacal others. But generally harmless. And about as deep as a mud puddle. We've spent a lot of years living in this skin and gotten used to it. This ain't a pair of those yuppie jeans that come already pre-distressed. That's cheating. Trust me on this one thing, if anything. No, as a rule, we've come to this point and know what we're about.

But a woman comes along.

At least, we should all be so lucky. She comes along and takes a fancy. And that's a good thing, because us poor slobs would be nowhere without her. Let's face it, Romeo'd have been just another dumb punk on the mean streets of Verona, but for a girl. They love us. Why, I don't know some days. But they flatter us. They let us open the pickle jar and make us kill spiders. But then they reach that magical moment when they decide that they can fix us.

Oh, they start out small and they mean well. And we look better for shaving every day and throwing out the old shirts with the holes in them. And sometimes we even clean up well enough not to embarrass them when they have a brand new dress and a whole party of people to stop dead. But they still mean to fix us. And we don't necessarily want to be fixed. Let's face it, you fix dogs, not boyfriends.

Men are all born with a subconscious understanding of entropy. That's why we turn into geeks and nerds and gearheads. It is that fundamental appreciation of a finely-tuned machine, purring at the peak of performance. And hell, we all love to tinker. Better. Stronger. Faster. Boys were raised to understand what that means. But at the end of the day, we change the things around us, while we try to stay the same carefree, rumpled guy we were in high school.

But a woman comes along.

Ladies, I don't think you even begin to appreciate how much you scare and intimidate us. But I suppose that if you did, that would make it even worse, so we'll let that one be for now. Never poke a sleeping bear.

A woman comes along. She lays claim to a man and takes that poor, grateful wretch and turns him into somebody. Maybe not somebody rich, or somebody famous, but somebody. Even if the value is only in her eyes and ours. And that's a good thing.

But a woman comes along.

What is it that's so wrong with us that we need fixing, anyway? What is that fundamental connection that goes on in your head that says, "I like him, but everything needs to change."? If you like us, can't that be enough? Do we need to be better? I suppose, to be fair, that one way to look at it is that where men turn to geekiness with machines, women express that same gene with their men. Better. Stronger. Faster. But you still scare us. Nobody ever asked the car if it wanted to be tuned.

I've given it a lot of thought over the years, on a lot of long, slow nights like this. Speaking as a guy, and thus categorically incapable of understanding the female mind, I can still only hazard a guess. What we geeks call a SWAG, a "Scientific Wild-Ass Guess." She's looking for a man who hasn't been too well trained yet, but has the potential to be turned into something good. Maybe even something special. Too much training, and she'll never get those fingerprints off of you from previous women. Not enough polish and she'll never make enough headway to justify the effort. And then he becomes a project, like the nerd's next computer, or the gearhead's next car, or the otaku's next costume. And that's when the irresistible force of her will meets the immoveable object of his ignorance.

I'll let you in on a little secret, ladies. We're lazy, not necessarily stubborn. We are resistant to change because we're unsure where it all leads. That leaves you with two options, once you've identified your victim and begun to swoop in for the kill. You can explain your motives and plan, and see how he reacts. The important part here is vagueness. I can't begin to tell you just how effective it is with us to start a paragraph off with, "Wouldn't it be cool if..."

The key is patience. A man won't immediately cotton to any idea. That's just us. But sneak it in a few times, carefully, and one morning you can act all surprised when he repeats it back to you word for word as an original idea. Don't be offended. It's a high compliment. It just takes a while to burrow through our thick skulls and take up residence.

The other option requires a great deal of sneakiness, and it's a good thing y'all aren't naturally sneaky creatures. Option two involves using your God-given gifts and a little blackmail. And more sneakiness. Rather than just telling us our wardrobe fails to pass muster, you have to drag us off to go shopping, with the goal of achieving one small success at a time. Show us three shirts, ones you've already sized, accessorized, and approved. And make us buy one. We're liable to pick any of them, just to escape shopping, but we'll pick one if you stick to it. Especially if you include something along the lines of, "This will go great with my new sexy dress I just bought." Throw in a flash of cleavage and a saucy roll of the rump, and we're likely to agree to anything. Sex really does sell.

And then you put the new shirt at the front of the closet. We're visual creatures. First thing we see in the closet is that shirt, and our brain immediately short-circuits back to the cleavage. Then you hide the old shirts at the back of the closet. Very slowly, one at a time, you take them out and hide them someplace. Be careful never to throw away the ones with great emotional attachment. That's the path to ruin. Men are pack rats with amazingly sophisticated mental filing systems. We won't miss something for years at a time, but we'll never forget the good ones. Especially after you go along a few years and now are recycling old ratty shirts that you originally bought us. It's still associated with cleavage, especially if you deposit just enough scent around to mark your territory. We were born hunters, and smell drives the deepest, strongest memories. Just a spritz of perfume across the whole closet. Enough that his subconscious locks on, but not enough that his brain ever engages. Like I said, deep as a mud puddle. And if the brain does come into play, he's liable to appreciate your effort, because obviously you care enough to scare off every other woman out there. You have to be sneaky.

But here is the million dollar question. After you've put this much effort and love into changing your man, are you even going to like him? Now that you've gone and transformed him into the person his mother always dreamt he'd be, to the point that his dog barely recognizes him, will he be someone you still like? Is it worth the end result of all this effort that got you to capture this poor wretch in the first place? Or is it the prize of finding a man you can mold and the challenge of renovating him? Once you're done with him, then what?

Remember, men don't like change. So setting out on this quest will be worse than slaying a dragon, and longer than reducing the walls of Ilium. Our single most cogent fear, the one that wakes us in the dead of night, is that we'll agree to become someone else, for your love, only to find that the Emerald City is all an illusion. That's why we get cynical and jaded. Trust me, I'm speaking from experience. We've done it, changed everything, and now you've changed your mind.

END OF PLAY

THE WINTERSTONE
A PLAY IN ONE ACT

Characters

Clarissa

Young woman. Up and coming musician. Sharp and smart. Raised poor.

West

Middle-aged, middle class man, widower.

Setting

Modern day. Front seat of a two-seater sports car.

Time

Late afternoon.

SCENE 1

At Rise: Both characters seated side by side in a two-seat sports car. WEST is driving. CLARISSA in passenger seat.

CLARISSA
I really want to thank you for stopping to help and giving me a ride. This is such a cute little car. You're sure we can make it to the club on time?

WEST
No problem at all. You did say nine o'clock, but it's only half seven now and shouldn't take more than 30 minutes to get there. You'll have plenty of time. But won't you need everyone else we just left back there?

CLARISSA
Them? No. The band, the DJ, and all the dancers are already at the club waiting for me to get there.

WEST

Then who was that mob?

CLARISSA

Those were my People.

WEST

Your "People?"

CLARISSA

That's right. Howard, my manager, had us stop at a radio station along the way for a publicity event. We were done with that and heading for the venue when the limo died. Never take shortcuts to save time.

WEST

Well, someone would have come along if I hadn't. They might have even had enough space for all of your, uhm, "people." Although, I suppose that might have taken a lorry. Howard. He was the one I nearly ran over?

CLARISSA

No, that was Rick, the logistics coordinator. Howard was the short, bald guy in back screaming into his cell phone.

WEST

Ah, the one with the inexplicably-large chin and the rather unfortunate suit.

CLARISSA

Ha. You know, I've never heard him described that way, but it fits. You sure getting me there isn't taking you out of your way?

WEST

I don't really have a way, so I don't know that you could be disturbing it.

CLARISSA
Really? Where were you headed tonight?

WEST
Eh? There really wasn't a where, so much as a why.

CLARISSA
I don't get it.

WEST
Have you ever had one of those days where you wake up and decide you don't want to go to work?

CLARISSA
All the time. Wish I could.

WEST
They've been on me for some time to use some of my vacation, and nothing was pressing, so I called in and let them know not to even bother taking messages for a few days.

CLARISSA
So you've just been out driving all day?

WEST
Actually, since Tuesday.

CLARISSA
Tuesday? Where?

WEST
Oh, here and there. I've been celebrating Rune's Rule.

CLARISSA
What is that?

WEST
To quote the man: "If you don't care where you're going, you're not lost." So, everywhere.

CLARISSA
God, that would be so nice.

WEST
You don't get to take a day off, even occasionally?

CLARISSA
I'm lucky if they give me an hour to myself. There's always somebody with something that can't wait. Rehearsals. Interviews. Songwriters. Accountants. Trainers. Publicity.

WEST
So, I take it you are a singer.

CLARISSA
I'm Clarissa. "Cla-RI-ssa."

WEST
Yes, I caught that much when (you said his name was Howard?) introduced you. But I didn't catch your last name.

CLARISSA
There is no last name, baby. Just Clarissa. Owner of the fastest-climbing dance hit on the radio. You've got to have heard of me.

WEST
Are you going to be mortally offended if I say no?

CLARISSA
Really?

WEST
Really.

CLARISSA
Man, what kind of radio stations do you listen to?

WEST

Apparently, the wrong ones.

CLARISSA

We need to fix that. How do you turn this thing on?

WEST

I'd rather you didn't.

CLARISSA

Don't you want to know?

WEST

I'm willing to take your word for it. I find it rather more soothing without any music. The hum of the highway is quite relaxing.

CLARISSA

What about news?

WEST

How often do you hear anything good happen? It's all just wars, taxes, and complaints about lying politicians.

CLARISSA

How do you stay in touch?

WEST

Don't really need to. Left the mobile turned off and sitting on the charger. It'll keep track for when I get back.

CLARISSA

What about your wife? Or girlfriend? I don't see a ring.

WEST

You were right the first time. Wife. Well, past tense.

CLARISSA

I'm sorry.

WEST

It's all right. Everyone always says that, followed by that same awkward silence. But it's been a while. Eventually, they say, the pain goes away.

CLARISSA

Does it?

WEST

I'm still waiting on that part. Let's just say it sneaks up on me less often these days. I still have icepick moments.

CLARISSA

Icepick moments?

WEST

That's when you think you've got everything sorted out, under control, and then suddenly something goes through all the layers and your heart goes cold.

CLARISSA

Like an icepick.

WEST

Most assuredly. I'll come around a corner and see someone, or hear a song that reminds me of her.

CLARISSA

That's why you leave the radio off?

WEST

Pretty much.

CLARISSA

And why you drive?

WEST

Like I said, it's not a where. It's more of a why.

CLARISSA
Well, I appreciate that you were there to ride up and rescue me. I really need this gig tonight. What's so funny?

WEST
It's been rather some time since I was someone's knight in shining armour, riding in to save the day.

CLARISSA
Tonight, you can be my Lancelot.

WEST
I was always more partial to Gawain, myself.

CLARISSA
Why's that?

WEST
Not as flashy as the rest. Came in, got the job done, went on his way. Minimum of fuss.

CLARISSA
(Snorts.)

WEST
Not your style, I take it?

CLARISSA
I'm all about fuss, honey. You gotta make a big splash. Shock people. Rattle cages. Make some big noise. Otherwise, they miss you and go on to the next big thing.

WEST
So you are, currently, the "Next Big Thing," I take it?

CLARISSA
That's right. I'm in all the dance halls, on all the radio stations. Baby, they can't get enough of me right now. Tonight's gonna be a

live feed and a packed house. I got 'em lined up around the corner waiting on little ol' me to light the fuse and bring the house down. You oughtta come.

WEST

Not really my cup of tea, I suspect. Rather more loud and exciting than my tastes normally run.

CLARISSA

We're gonna have to expand your horizons, I see.

WEST

That's rather what I was doing when I stumbled across your mob, your, uhm, "People," broken down and standing in the middle of the road back there.

CLARISSA

More like running away, you ask me.

WEST

How so?

CLARISSA

Just pack up and drive aimlessly? Nobody else? No mobile? What about your friends?

WEST

I don't really have that many close friends.

CLARISSA

Why not?

WEST

I don't really know.

CLARISSA

It's because you keep people at a distance. Mister Quiet Serious. Sir Gawain. Isn't that the one? Come in, get the job done, minimum of fuss? Nobody to harsh your smooth?

WEST

Well, I suppose so, if I understand your vernacular correctly.

CLARISSA

Honey, you need more riot in your life. A whole lotta noise and energy.

WEST

Like that mob back there?

CLARISSA

Sugar, you don't know the half of it. I got six brothers and sisters. I try to talk to my mom every day, and if we ever get back to civilization and I can recharge my phone, I bet I got a hundred messages in the last three hours, from my sisters, my cousins, my friends.

WEST

Wasn't that the same life you mentioned wanting to escape from?

CLARISSA

That was the tour I need a break from. On top of all my family, I got all these people who want a piece of me. Every day. They're just bloodsuckers. Them's the ones I could do without.

WEST

Quite.

CLARISSA

I gotta tell you, though, it's kinda nice not having the phone ring, and nobody telling me to hurry. So you might have something there, dude. You know, I don't even know your name, Sir Gawain.

WEST

Actually, that's as good as anything. It's not like I'll grow confused as to whom you might be talking.

CLARISSA

No, seriously, man. It would weird me out calling you Sir Gawain all night.

WEST

In that case, my name is West.

CLARISSA

West? As in the direction?

WEST

As in the direction.

CLARISSA

How'd you get that one? You take "Go west, young man" a little too serious?

WEST

Actually, my mother named me Westmoreland.

CLARISSA

Seriously?

WEST

Yes, ma'am.

CLARISSA

Wow. Heavy. West it is.

WEST

Thank you.

CLARISSA

You got a last name, West?

WEST

I don't see that that's fair, Clarissa. You haven't got one.

CLARISSA

Ouch. OK. Ya got me there. So, if it's not too personal, what was her name? Your wife.

WEST

Sophie.

CLARISSA

Sophie. That's a pretty name. How long were you two together?

WEST

Near eleven years.

CLARISSA

Wow. Kids?

WEST

No.

CLARISSA

Why not?

WEST

Hmmm?

CLARISSA

How come you never had kids? You were together for so long.

WEST

It's hard to say. I suppose we were just busy doing things. We talked about it, but the time was never right. That's always something you're going to do next year, after things settle down.

CLARISSA

But they never did?

WEST

They never do. I suppose that's something you have to make happen, rather than letting it solve itself. But, on balance, it's probably just as well.

CLARISSA
Why's that?

WEST
I have enough trouble dealing with it myself. I can't imagine trying to explain to children that their mother is going away and never coming back.

CLARISSA
That would suck.

WEST
Indeed, but I'm glad that I got the time with her that I did. That the good was so much better than the bad.

CLARISSA
Man. Eleven years. That's like, forever. How'd you manage it?

WEST
Manage? It's nothing, really, when you're in love. And it goes by like a single day. One you can never get back, once it's gone. You haven't been so lucky?

CLARISSA
Hardly.

WEST
No beau? Nobody special in that mob back there? No one waiting for you after the show? Nobody back home? Never been bit by the bug?

CLARISSA
No. Well, not really. I mean. It's complicated.

WEST
That sounds rather definitive.

CLARISSA

It's like. There was. A boy, I mean. But things were just starting to break for me. And I had to leave. And he wasn't in to it all. The travel and the tours and the stuff.

WEST

He wouldn't come?

CLARISSA

He told me if I really loved him, I'd give it up and stay with him.

WEST

How did this fool take "No."?

CLARISSA

West, I've wanted this more than anything in my life. Since I was five. My mom has videos of me singing along to the radio, holding a hairbrush like a mic.

WEST

I'll let you in on a secret, Clarissa. All moms do.

CLARISSA

Really? Your mom has a video of you doing that?

WEST

No comment.

CLARISSA

Uh huh.

WEST

So this young man, I take it he stayed entirely behind?

CLARISSA

Said he couldn't see himself singing backup or carrying turntables. Just walked away. It's like he never loved me at all.

WEST
His loss. Do you ever talk to him?

CLARISSA
Not so much anymore. I've been busy with the music, and then the business. Any more, there really nothing much to say.

WEST
If he asked you to give up your dreams instead of finding a way to help you achieve them, then you are probably much better off without him around.

CLARISSA
Yeah. My sister said he settled down with some little cheerleader chicka and started popping out babies. She was always kinda dumb. The girl, not my sister. Well, her too, but not as bad.

WEST
And she is probably getting exactly what she wants out of life without giving him too much of a challenge.

CLARISSA
Would you have done something like that, if Sophie'd have asked?

WEST
Dropped everything and gone off on some adventure?

CLARISSA
For her?

WEST
You mean like: selling the house, putting the cars in storage, and living on a sailboat for a year?

CLARISSA
You did that?

WEST
Yes. It was her idea.

CLARISSA
When was that?

WEST
Right after we found out she was sick.

CLARISSA
Wait. After?

WEST
Yes, after. The doctor told us that there was nothing much he could do. She had perhaps six months, maybe, and that it would be relatively painless up until almost the very end.

CLARISSA
Six months? But you went sailing for a year? How long was she sick?

WEST
Just shy three years.

CLARISSA
Then what did you do?

WEST
After that? Hmm. Learned the Argentinean Tango. Then she took up painting.

CLARISSA
Wow.

WEST
Young lady, tomorrow is implied, never promised. You live each day as if it's your last, hoping to be wrong. And every morning you give thanks to be wrong, because one of these days you won't be.

And if that young man couldn't see what you really wanted, then he didn't love you at all. And you need to find another young man who will.

CLARISSA

Thank you. But what about you?

WEST

How's that?

CLARISSA

What are you doing these days to celebrate her life? Or yours? It sounds to me like you keep everyone at a distance, and hide from the world. You brood. And when the brooding boils over, you drive until it all goes away. Trust me. I understand brooding.

WEST

I'm damaged goods. I lost my soul when I lost her.

CLARISSA

But you get up the next morning and keep going. Somebody told me that recently.

WEST

I don't know how. I've forgotten.

CLARISSA

How do you forget how to live?

WEST

You forget how to live alone. After that long, some things atrophy because you've always done them WITH someone. FOR someone. When you wake up one morning without that someone, there's a piece ripped out of your soul. I hope you never have to live through that, because that morning was the hardest day I've ever faced. You get up, look in the mirror, and have to ask yourself, "What do I do with the rest of my life?"

CLARISSA

And?

WEST

And nobody answers.

CLARISSA

I'm sorry.

WEST

It's all right. Nobody understands except the ones that have been there. And they don't need to say anything.

CLARISSA

You survived.

WEST

Oh, aye. And I brood. And when the darkness gets to be too much, I drive. And then it goes away for a while.

CLARISSA

Icepick moments.

WEST

Icepick moments.

CLARISSA

So you need to reinvent yourself.

WEST

Oh, I've tried starting over. But it's rough and painful. And does not seem to be working.

CLARISSA

I don't mean starting over. I mean leaving it all behind and becoming someone new.

WEST

How so?

CLARISSA

My mom used to tell me a fairie tale about the Winterstone.

WEST

Winterstone?

CLARISSA

Winterstone. It goes something like this. There was this group of heroes, searching for gold, and princesses, and dragons. That sort of thing.

WEST

Okay.

CLARISSA

So one day, they came to the very edge of the world, at a place called Land's End. In front of them was just water forever, and no one knew what was on the other side. These men were already famous, and rich, and loved by everyone, but they wanted to know what was out there. So they built a ship on the beach, made a pact, and sat a plinth. All of their names were carved into it, and they lit a candle at the base. Then they sailed off, over the horizon, and were never heard from again. When other people came to settle the area, they found the memorial and called it the Winterstone.

WEST

So what's that got to do with me? I should reinvent myself by building a boat and sailing into the sunset?

CLARISSA

Something like that. Become someone new.

WEST

Rather like the Hellenes, in reverse, then.

CLARISSA

The who?

WEST

When an ancient Greek army crossed the ocean, their king ordered all of the boats burned when they landed. That way, everyone understood that there could be no retreat. The choices were victory or death.

CLARISSA

Yeah, just like that. You need to build a Winterstone for Sophie.

WEST

For Sophie?

CLARISSA

Yes. All your good memories. And your love. And then you set it up on a beach so that everyone who comes along after can see what a wonderful woman she was. I think I need to write a song about her.

WEST

How? You never knew her.

CLARISSA

I don't need to. You did. I can see how much you loved her, just looking at you when you talk about her. I want that in my life.

WEST

It's a two-edged sword.

CLARISSA

They all are, baby. But I've only ever had the bad edge. I didn't realize what the good part could be like. Thank you. Now I know.

WEST

No, thank you. I think I can let go of some of the harder bits now.

CLARISSA
No more icepick moments?

WEST
Oh, God, no. I hope those never go away.

CLARISSA
Wait. Why not?

WEST
Because they remind me just how much I loved her. What a wonderful woman she was. I don't ever want to lose that.

CLARISSA
Wow. I never thought of it that way.

WEST
Neither had I. I just had my love for her. And missing her. I think I know how to let go. At least enough to get on.

CLARISSA
See, there was a reason why the car broke down when it did.

WEST
Come again?

CLARISSA
He moves in dark and mysterious ways, West. We were supposed to meet there, so you could overcome your own darkness.

WEST
And you? What was His purpose for you today?

CLARISSA
He wanted me to see what it was to be truly loved by someone. Unconditionally. Irrevocably.

WEST
You've never seen it?

CLARISSA
Well, I guess my parents love each other, but...

WEST
But they are your parents. And that makes it very hard to see them as two love-struck teenagers, doesn't it?

CLARISSA
You understand.

WEST
Oh, yes. My parents have been married for fifty-six years and still hold hands when they go for a walk.

CLARISSA
See, that's what I'm talking about. Why can't something like that happen to me?

WEST
Because you weren't ready for it.

CLARISSA
What do you mean?

WEST
Talking about absolute, eternal love. Would you have recognized it? You've never known what it looked like. It's not the princess in the fairie tale tower. It's being there for someone when the times are as bad as they'll ever get. Not just when they are as good as they can be. It means not doing something you wanted to, because your partner doesn't want to. It means doing something you hate, just to see the smile on their face. It means being there. It means finding a space, in the middle of unhappiness, where you both can be happy. Walking in the rain, holding hands, is just the icing on the cake. It's hard work.

CLARISSA

But you did it? You had it?

WEST

Yes. I did.

CLARISSA

That means I can get it.

WEST

When you're ready for it, it tends to sneak up and bites you on the arse.

CLARISSA

But I have to give things up?

WEST

Being in love means carving out a space for someone else in your life and making everyone else respect that. At that point, you aren't losing anything. Quite the contrary. It becomes something bigger. And it's not that big of a sacrifice.

CLARISSA

All the same, I just can't lose my focus. The music won't wait.

WEST

Even if some guy comes along who might be the right one?

CLARISSA

Like you said, if he's the right one, really the right one, then I'll know, and he'll be willing to wait until the music is done with me.

WEST

Done with you?

CLARISSA

Nobody lasts very long in this business. I got, maybe, five years tops, if I'm lucky, before things completely change. After that, I'm probably washed up and forgotten.

WEST
So you can't make a career of it? Some do.

CLARISSA
Less than one in a thousand. But I'm gonna make a go of it. I just might make it. If not, I still want to make my rock.

WEST
Then what?

CLARISSA
Then I'll be a twenty-eight-year-old has-been thrown to the side of the road.

WEST
Why do it?

CLARISSA
Gimme five years and I can make enough to retire a long time and still die rich.

WEST
Really?

CLARISSA
Really.

WEST
Is it worth it? If that young man isn't willing to wait years?

CLARISSA
You've never been poor, have you? Really poor?

WEST
No, I suppose not.

CLARISSA

Then you don't understand what someone would be willing to give up to not be poor anymore.

WEST

Even happiness?

CLARISSA

Already done that. A few years won't matter. There are always other fish out there.

WEST

Just don't give up anything you'll regret losing. Five years might sound like forever, and, God forbid, thirty sounds ancient right now, but some things you can never get back, no matter how hard you try.

CLARISSA

Like love?

WEST

Love is easy. Regret. Losing something and always wondering if that was the right choice. It's like losing a tooth. You keep probing the hole in your life.

CLARISSA

So I should give up music for love?

WEST

Absolutely not. But you should consider giving up the plan if something good comes along. Be prepared to actually be happy when you can, rather than "someday." There's quite a lot of road to explore on the other side of thirty. Trust me on that one. Maybe you can leave your own Winterstone.

CLARISSA

Happy, huh?

WEST
I know. Heaven forbid you should smile occasionally and actually enjoy yourself while working so hard to have fun. I was young once. I remember.

CLARISSA
You aren't THAT old.

WEST
It's not the years. It's the miles.

CLARISSA
Uh huh. Old man, all withered up?

WEST
Something like that.

CLARISSA
But you're going to try as well, right?

WEST
I shall endeavor, Clarissa. You have given me a reason to believe it possible.

CLARISSA
Like I said, He moves in mysterious ways.

WEST
Yes, indeed he does. Now, I shall drop you here, young lady. One backstage door and an apparently frantic venue manager.

CLARISSA
So, after all this, you aren't going to come in and see the show?

WEST
Oh, I think we've about covered everything. If we leave it here, you can go back to being you and I'll keep looking for the far side of that horizon.

CLARISSA

You sure?

WEST

Why spoil perfection?

CLARISSA

You know, you're the first man in five years who hasn't tried to hit on me.

WEST

Really? Well, sorry to spoil your streak. But, perhaps you should look at it as an opportunity for that fresh start. I believe you've earned it.

CLARISSA

On one condition.

WEST

For you? Anything.

CLARISSA

Kiss me.

WEST

I beg your pardon?

CLARISSA

You heard me.

WEST

Well, yes. Why?

CLARISSA

You haven't kissed a woman since you lost her, have you? I mean really kissed her and meant it.

WEST
No, I don't suppose I have.

CLARISSA
So kiss me, and you can remember what it's like. You gave me a fresh start. This can be yours.

WEST
But what if someone sees? Won't that be bad?

CLARISSA
Gawain, there's no such thing as bad publicity in this business. If they do see, all they can do is wonder. The more they talk about it, the more they're talking about me. I certainly won't tell them anything.

WEST
What if someone recognizes me?

CLARISSA
Then you're going to have one hell of a good story to tell everyone when you get back. If you want to.

WEST
You are a much deeper woman, a much older woman, than you appear.

CLARISSA
This business ages you fast, if you're gonna survive.

WEST
Well, then. Perhaps you can be Sleeping Beauty, Miss Clarissa.

CLARISSA
I think I'd like that. Now kiss me.

(They KISS.) (Note: Long and romantic, but not passionate.)

CLARISSA
(Opens car door. Gets out. EXIT. House dark.)

(As lights fade, sound of a car engine revving up, and then fading.)

END OF PLAY

APPENDIX: 'Song of the Lost'

first: the Winterstone Chronicles

And in the fading autumn sunlight
I gathered my brothers together
a glance back to the lands lost
and then fore into the gathering gloom
there lay our destiny
to claim those lands from the darkness
those of us that survived

Come morning the company had dwindled
somewhere behind us were homesteads
roads and cities springing up
where our feet had trod
and our brothers stopped

Desert-scarred we came
riding out of the dawn into a new world
grim and silent save for the horses and tack
rugged faces carved by storm and sun
eyes both dead and blazing

Before us stretched an ocean to infinity
mocking us with calm regard
I remembered the ancient Muslim call
that we stop only because there exists no ford
to cross that ocean
as Allah must bear witness
but my army
small in number and mighty in vision
would not be swayed by distance
not after the desert

We built a boat
and sent the horses back to nature
facing a new desert
eternal in its emptiness
as dangerous as the stone behind

On the last cliff face
overlooking the sea
each of us carved a single line
a memorial and a stone
for the day the sons of lost brothers came
at its base we lit a candle
remaking the pact borne of fire
a circle of grim angry faces
brothers joined in purpose facing the darkness
and set out for our destiny

--Song of the Lost,
Winterstone Memorial, Land's End

About the Author

Blaze Ward writes science fiction in the Alexandria Station universe: The Jessica Keller Chronicles, The Science Officer series, The Doyle Iwakuma Stories, and others. He also writes about The Collective as well as The Fairchild Stories and Modern Gods superhero myths. You can find out more at his website www.blazeward.com, as well as Facebook, Goodreads, and other places.

Blaze's works are available as ebooks, paper, and audio, and can be found at a variety of online vendors (Kobo, Amazon, iBooks, and others). His newsletter comes out quarterly, and you can also follow his blog on his website. He really enjoys interacting with fans, and looks forward to any and all questions-even ones about his books!

Never miss a release!
If you'd like to be notified of new releases, sign up for my newsletter.

I only send out newsletters once a quarter, will never spam you, or use your email for nefarious purposes. You can also unsubscribe at any time.
http://www.blazeward.com/newsletter/

About Knotted Road Press

Knotted Road Press fiction specializes in dynamic writing set in mysterious, exotic locations.

Knotted Road Press non-fiction publishes autobiographies, business books, cookbooks, and how-to books with unique voices.

Knotted Road Press creates DRM-free ebooks as well as high-quality print books for readers around the world.

With authors in a variety of genres including literary, poetry, mystery, fantasy, and science fiction, Knotted Road Press has something for everyone.

Knotted Road Press
www.KnottedRoadPress.com

www.ingramcontent.com/pod-product-compliance
Lightning Source LLC
Chambersburg PA
CBHW070053120526
44588CB00033B/1422